A guide Lyme Regis & Bridport

by Robert Hesketh

Inspiring Places Publishing
2 Down Lodge Close
Alderholt
Fordingbridge
SP6 3JA

ISBN 978-1-8384668-1-7
www.inspiringplaces.co.uk

©Robert Hesketh 2021
www.roberthesketh.co.uk
All rights reserved
Contains Ordnance Survey data © Crown copyright and database right (2011)

Contents

Introduction … 3

Lyme Regis … 4

Charmouth … 17

Whitchurch Canonicorum … 19

Chideock, Seatown and Golden Cap … 20

Symondsbury … 21

Bridport … 23

West Bay … 33

Calendar of main events in Lyme and Bridport … 39

Two interesting walks … 40

Introduction

Bridport and Lyme Regis on Dorset's Jurassic Coast are small, but exceptionally attractive and interesting towns, with a great deal to offer visitors. Lyme is best known for its beaches and pretty harbour sheltered by its long, curving breakwater, the Cobb. Along with Charmouth, Lyme is internationally renowned for its fossils and its place in the development of geology and our understanding of evolution and the Earth's history.

The natural beauty of Lyme, the Cobb and the narrow streets lined with historic buildings will be recognizable to many through literature and cinema, especially Jane Austen's *Persuasion* and John Fowles's *The French Lieutenant's Woman*. Use this guide to explore the town in the footsteps of Anne Elliot, Sarah Woodruff et al and discover its remarkable ammonite pavement, its museums, fossil shops, working mill, galleries and artists' workshops.

Bridport too is ideal for exploration on foot. Like Lyme, its central area is compact with a great architectural heritage and a choice of cafés, restaurants and inns offering a wide variety of refreshment from light snacks to full meals. There is much to discover, including the arts centre, museum, theatres and Art Deco cinema. West Bay, Bridport's historic harbour, is a delight to explore too. Also included in this guide are Charmouth, Seatown and Eype on the dramatic Jurassic Coast between Lyme and West Bay, plus the exceptionally attractive inland villages of Symondsbury, Burton Bradstock, Whitchurch Canonicorum and Chideock.

The harbour at Lyme Regis.

Lyme Regis

The Iron Age settlement at Holcombe near Uplyme was later built over with a small Roman villa, but the earliest record of Lyme itself was in a charter of AD 774, when land on the west bank of the river Lim (a Celtic word for stream) was granted to Sherborne Abbey. This settlement was probably very small and consisted of salt makers who supplied salt to the abbey.

By the time of the Domesday survey (1086), Lyme was a growing community of 43 households based on salt and fishing. It added Regis to its name on becoming a royal manor during Edward I's reign. Edward granted Lyme its first royal charter in 1284, giving it two Members of Parliament. However, Lyme had been trading wine and wool before then and had a market from 1250, much to the chagrin of its trading rival, Bridport. Lyme emerged as the pre-eminent harbour between Exmouth and Weymouth after its rival port, Axmouth, declined following a cliff fall and silting of the river Axe.

Lyme becomes a major port: the Cobb

Lyme's development as a major port was only possible because of the Cobb, the remarkable, curving breakwater which makes Lyme's otherwise exposed and dangerous beach a harbour. The first record of the Cobb dates from 1313, when Edward I made a grant for its repair after storm damage.

Thus the Cobb must have existed from at least the late 13th century. Repairs after further storm damage followed in 1377. Lyme's builders gained a national reputation for their ingenuity in floating large "cowstones" supported by barrels into position and holding them in place with huge oak stakes. Further repairs in 1545 called for 61 new oak trunks.

Lyme Regis, the Cobb.

Lyme Regis, looking east towards Charmouth.

Repairing the Cobb has been a constant theme in Lyme's history, but the heavy cost was amply repaid. In the late 16th century Thomas Gerard noted:

The town flourisheth, well built, and enriched by the Convenience of the Cobb, which is an Harbour that the Inhabitants, with much Industrie and Charge, have built by the sea, by pileing together great Rocks, which at low water with empty Caskes they weigh up, and by this means have made the Harbour safe for Barkes of good Burthen to ride in: for the better repairing and enlarging of which, they choose yearly two Overseers, whom they call Cobwardens, whose office is to see the Cobb well repaired of those Breaches, which manie times the Sea makes in it.

Hemmed in by high cliffs east and west, Lyme could only expand inland. Nonetheless, it was a substantial port by 1332, assessed just behind Dorset's leading port, Weymouth. As further proof of its vitality, Lyme provided four ships and 62 mariners for the Calais siege in 1347, compared with five ships and 96 men from Portsmouth.

Despite French raids, the plague and a terrible storm in 1377 that destroyed the Cobb, 80 houses and 50 ships, Lyme showed great resilience and continued to prosper. When Leland visited around 1540 he found ...*a praty market town, set in the rootes of an high rokky hill down to the hard shore. This town hath good shippes and usith fishing and merchauntice. Merchauntes of Morleys (Morlaix in Brittany) much haunt this town.*

Trading with Africa, the Mediterranean, America and the West Indies, Lyme exported cloth and manufactures and imported ivory and redwood dyes. By the early 17th century, Lyme was paying £5,000 annually in

The harbour, Lyme Regis.

port taxes. However, the port could not handle ships larger than 150 tons and thus lost trade as vessels grew larger. Simultaneously, the West of England's woollen and cloth industry declined, largely moving to the North.

Nonetheless, the Cobb was rebuilt in mortared masonry in the 18th century. The government recognized its strategic importance as the only protected harbour along a dangerous stretch of coast at a time of threatened French invasion and footed the repair bill when the Cobb was badly damaged in 1792. Lt Colonel Fanshawe made further repairs in 1818, returning after the Great Storm of 1824 to repair 232ft of pier and 447ft of parapet.

Fanshawe's repairs have stood the test of time and enabled Lyme to continue as a commercial port, with an average of 600 vessels docking annually in the early 19th century. Although international trade increasingly transferred to deep water ports, the Cobb remained vital in protecting Lyme's coastal, fishing and leisure trades. It also continued to shelter shipbuilding at Lyme, which began in the 13th century and, although in decline, still produced over a hundred vessels in the 19th century, including its largest ever, the full rigged *Salacia*, 475 tons, in 1853.

Lyme in the Civil War

Fiercely Puritan, Lyme was ardent for Parliament and defied a two month long Royalist siege by Prince Maurice's 6,000 men in 1644. Despite being heavily outnumbered and bombarded with fire arrows and red hot cannon balls, the defenders enjoyed the very great advantages of being defended by the Cobb and supplied by Parliament's dominant navy. Moreover, the garrison of 600 and the townsmen – bravely supported by their womenfolk who loaded their muskets – were ably led by Lt Colonel Robert Blake, who later rose to be Cromwell's General at Sea.

Lyme and the Monmouth Rebellion, 1685

Knowing of Lyme's heroism in 1644 and its strong anti-Papist tradition, James, Duke of Monmouth chose to land there on June 11th, 1685 on what is now Monmouth Beach with three small ships, four light field guns and a mere 82 supporters. Posing as the Protestant champion to wrest the throne from his Catholic uncle James I, this illegitimate son of Charles II could further count on resentment in Lyme at the imposition of Royalist Gregory Alford as Mayor in 1684. Alford persecuted local Baptists, Independents and Quakers, forcing them to worship in secret. White Chapel Rocks in the Undercliff was one clandestine meeting place for local Nonconformists.

By June 15th Monmouth had gained over a thousand men, including an estimated third of the men of Lyme. Although poorly armed, this largely amateur force gained some initial successes against local militia. Perhaps inevitably, they met defeat from King James's better trained and equipped forces at Sedgemoor, Somerset on July 6th. Some 1,500 men who had joined the would-be usurper were killed out of over 3,500. The survivors were hunted and taken prisoner.

Many of Monmouth's adherents were tried by the infamous Judge Jeffreys and condemned to transportation or death. Twelve local men were hanged on Monmouth Beach. Eleven of them were quartered too and their tarred remains hung about the town as a hideous warning. (One man escaped quartering after his sister bribed Jeffreys with £1,000).

Monmouth Beach.

Jane Austen's Lyme: *Persuasion*

Jane Austen visited Lyme in 1803 and 1804. Britain was at war with France and continental travel was impossible. Thus attractive English seaside towns such as Lyme were beginning to develop as genteel resorts, following the lead set by Weymouth and Brighton, popularized by George III and the Prince of Wales respectively.

Lyme made a vivid impression on Jane, who set much of her last novel, *Persuasion* (1817) here. Whereas most places in her novels can only be visited in the imagination, Lyme (like Bath) is described vividly and accurately. *Persuasion's* narrator states: "A very strange stranger it must be who does not see charms in the immediate environs of Lyme, to make him wish to know it better…these places must be visited, and visited again to make the worth of Lyme understood."

Admirers of *Persuasion* duly came visiting, including Poet Laureate Alfred Tennyson, who went straight to the Cobb exclaiming "Show me the exact spot where Louisa Musgrove fell!"

With its many historic buildings, Lyme readily lends itself to costume drama. BBC's 1995 production of *Persuasion* with Amanda Root as Anne Elliot and Ciaran Hinds as Captain Wentworth was partly shot at Lyme, as was ITV's reprise in 2007 with Sally Hawkins and Rupert Penry Jones. Netflix viewers may soon see a new production starring Dakota Johnson which was being filmed on the Cobb whilst this book was being written in 2021. Yet another version of *Persuasion* with Sarah Snook in the lead role is planned.

During her stay in Lyme, Jane enjoyed walking on the Cobb, bathing (despite it being November), dancing at the Assembly Rooms and exploring Uplyme and Charmouth. If she could return today, she would no doubt be amused by the Jane Austen Gardens behind Marine Parade. She would readily recognize the Royal Lion in Broad Street and the Walk, now part of the longer and improved Marine Parade, where the cottages named after Captains Harville and Benwick date from about 1830. However, the Assembly Rooms are now occupied by Cobb Gate car park.

The characters in *Persuasion* arrive in Lyme by road, which was only possible after 1759. Before then, only tracks led to Lyme, which relied heavily on the sea for its trade and supplies and wheeled traffic was virtually unknown. Through the 19th century roads speeded Lyme's development as a resort, whilst the remarkable fossil discoveries of Mary Anning drew much attention to the town.

Mary Anning and fossil collecting

Lyme born fossil hunter Mary Anning (1799-1847) directly found or pointed the way to nearly every specimen of importance in palaeontology according to renowned palaeontologist Stephen Jay Gould. Science thus owes a huge debt to her dedicated collecting. Mary's work was largely done in winter, when landslips around Lyme reveal new fossils. Working quickly, she gathered her finds before the sea could claim them and thankfully survived the landslip that killed her dog in 1833. Despite her gender, humble background and modest education, her discoveries, including the first ichthyosaur to be correctly identified and the first two plesiosaur skeletons ever found, gained the attention of Henry Thomas De la Beche and William Buckland, two leading geologists of the time. She thus contributed to fundamental changes in scientific thinking, especially about the Earth's age, origins and development.

The ammonite pavement, Monmouth Beach.

Lyme's Development as a popular resort

Tourism at Lyme gained a huge boost when the branch railway from Axminster was opened, making travel much faster and cheaper and day excursions from far afield possible. Summer weekends saw heavy traffic, with many through carriages from London.

The line was not completed until 1903, long after most of Britain's railway network, due to Devon/Dorset border's hilly terrain. It was very steeply graded and sharply curved, with a 203 yard long mass concrete viaduct over Cannington Lane between the A3052 and Uplyme. Still extant, it is 92 feet high with ten arches of 50 foot span.

Lyme in literature and cinema

The powerful, enigmatic image of Sarah Woodruff standing on the Cobb in a black hooded cape from John Fowles' *The French Lieutenant's Woman* is indelibly associated with Lyme. Fowles' novel was filmed on location in 1981 with Meryl Streep as Sarah and Jeremy Irons as Charles Smithson, her obsessed and frustrated lover.

Fowles abandoned London in 1965 to live in the Undercliff west of Lyme at Underhill Farm, which features in both story and film. He spent the rest of his life in Lyme, becoming Honorary Curator of Lyme Regis Museum and writing a short history of the town (see Bibliography).

Mary Anning is the central character in Tracey Chevalier's *Remarkable Creatures* (2009), which gives a vivid depiction of 19th century Lyme. Strongly biographical, the novel explores the productive relationship between Mary and fellow fossil collector, Elizabeth Philpott.

Mary and Elizabeth Philpott are played by Katherine Hamilton and Jenny Agutter in "Mary Anning and the Dinosaur Hunters", a two part film directed by Sharon Sheehan and shot on location. Mary Anning is also the focus of interest in "Ammonite". Filmed in and around Lyme in 2019, it stars Kate Winslet as Mary Anning and Saoirse Ronan as her lover.

J.R.R. Tolkien was inspired by Lyme, where he spent childhood summers between 1905 and 1910. Returning in 1927 and 1928, Tolkien produced a great number of illustrations for his fantasy writing. Possibly, the Dorset countryside inspired the Shire in *Lord of the Rings* and *The Hobbit*.

Beatrix Potter drew Lyme and the countryside around in 1904 and

The Cobb from above.

later used some of her Lyme sketches in *The Tale of Little Pig Robinson*. The story is set in "Stymouth", a fictional seaside town strongly resembling Lyme.

Born in Lyme in 1804, John Gould became known internationally for his scientific work and beautifully illustrated bird books. In 1836 Charles Darwin bought Gould specimens from his Beagle voyage and studied Gould's paper on "The Transmutation of Species". Darwin published his seminal *On the Origin of Species* 23 years later.

Marine Parade, Lyme Regis.

Exploring Lyme
Monmouth beach, where the Duke of Monmouth landed in 1685 (page 7), is easily accessed from the Cobb car park. It stretches over a kilometre (¾ mile) west from the Cobb and is great for exploring (dogs are allowed). Although pebbles predominate, there is some sand at low tide, which also reveals the remarkable ammonite pavement at the western end. This spectacular fossil graveyard contains the remains of countless ammonites, an extinct group of marine molluscs that thrived 200 million years ago. Coroniceras, the main species, is commonly the size of a dinner plate. According to the Natural History Museum, this fossil ledge is unique.

Fossil hunt,ing
Belemnites are another common fossil on Monmouth Beach, Lyme's East Beach and Charmouth. Fossilized parts of a cuttlefish they, like ammonites, died out at the end of the Cretaceous Period (circa 66 million years ago), and are popularly known as "Thunderbolts" or "Thunder Bullets" from their smallness and slender, conical shape.

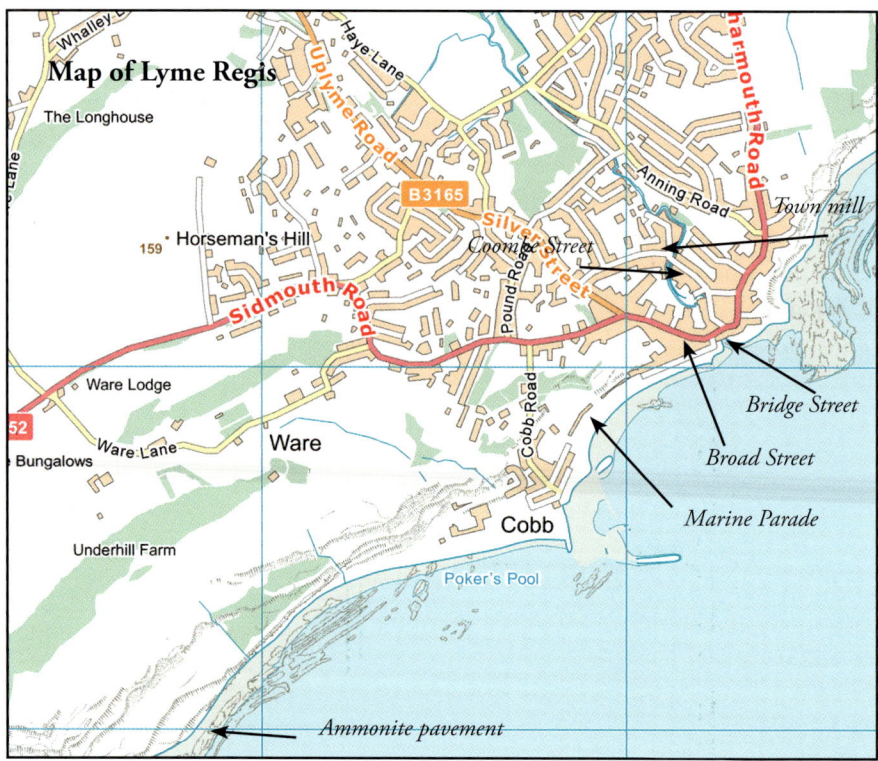

By the same token, the gnarled, curved fossilized shells of Gryphea, an extinct bivalve, are known as "Devil's Toenails". "Fairy Loaves" is the popular name for the small heart shaped fossilized shells of an ancient sea urchin. *Fossil hunting is very rewarding, particularly in winter when the beaches are quieter and the fossils more plentiful. For safety, please visit on a low (preferably a falling) tide and stay well clear of the notoriously unstable cliffs, especially those on Lyme's East Beach. Also, beware of slippery rocks, deep mud and the returning tide. Follow the fossil collecting code: leave the fossils embedded in the ammonite pavement (it is an SSSI) and do not dig into the cliffs without permission. Any extremely rare fossils should be reported to the Charmouth Heritage Coast Centre. The best way to begin is with one of the fossil hunting expeditions organized by experienced collectors from both Lyme and Charmouth. Contact Lyme Regis TIC 01297 442138; Lyme Regis Museum (page 14) 01297 443370 or Charmouth Heritage Coast Centre (page 17) 01297 560772 for more details.

The Cobb

To a large extent, the story of Lyme is the story of the Cobb (pages 4 to 6), which also offers the best views of Lyme and Lyme Bay. Start from the

Lifeboat Shop and Station, home to *Spirit of Loch Fyne*, an Atlantic 85 class inshore lifeboat, one of the RNLI's fastest lifeboats. Established in 1826, the station has a long and distinguished record, including 20 awards for gallantry. Opposite are various boards advertising boat trips, fishing trips, gig racing, water skiing, wakeboarding and more besides. Leisure craft and fishing boats share the harbour, best seen as the tide rises.

Lyme Regis Aquarium

Housed in one of the Cobb's early 18th century warehouses is Lyme Regis Aquarium, unique on the South Coast in holding a collection of locally found fish and marine creatures. Species on display include lobster, sea scorpions, blennies, ballan wrasse, dogfish, bass, mullet, starfish and crab. Interactive events include hand feeding the grey mullet, holding a starfish and getting close up to crabs. The Aquarium also shows short videos of dolphins in Lyme Bay, underwater footage of Lyme Bay's reef and dramatic scenes from the storms of 2014 battering the Cobb. The walls are covered in illustrated plaques describing Lyme's maritime heritage. On the wall outside is the 1879 toll board, detailing taxes levied on imports and exports to the harbour. (01297 444230 www.lymeregismarineaquarium.co.uk)

Marine Parade

After exploring the Cobb, walk by Front Beach, a delightful family friendly beach with fine sand and shallow water for children to play in. Maybe stop for refreshment at one of the beachside stalls or at the Royal Standard. The pub has low beamed ceilings taken from old ships and a fine Georgian front. Continue into Marine Parade with its attractive medley of mainly 19th cen-

Front Beach.

Front Beach from the Cobb.

tury buildings. Several are thatched and one has a fine sundial. At the far end is a plaque commemorating the US 16th Infantry Regiment, billeted in and around Lyme in 1943/44 in preparation for D Day. Cross Cobb Gate car park and turn right into Bridge Street.

Bridge Street

In 1915 HMS *Formidable* was torpedoed by German submarines and 540 men were lost. Survivors were brought to the Pilot Boat Inn and cared for. One sailor taken for dead was brought back to consciousness when Lassie, the landlord's dog, licked his face. It is probably no coincidence she bore the same name as the heroine of Eric Knight's 1940 novel *Lassie Come Home*, filmed in 1943.

Across the river Lim is the Fossil Shop with a wide range of fossils from local beaches and around the world. Opposite is the Guildhall, rebuilt in 1887, but incorporating 16th and 17th century fittings from its predecessor. Next is the museum.

Lyme Regis Museum

Described as "remarkable… a gem" by Sir David Attenborough, the museum presents Lyme and its history with excellent fossil collections; maritime and domestic objects; paintings, prints, archive photographs and much more besides. The interactive geological gallery in the Mary Anning Wing and the new Learning Centre are particularly good. Also of note is the room devoted to literary Lyme, the audio visual displays and a stunning view of Lyme Bay. (01297 443370 www.lymeregismusuem.co.uk)

Marine Theatre

Turn right out of the Museum, left into Church Street and right through the arch for the Marine Theatre, which offers a lively programme of plays, cinema, music, community events and talks. Retrace your steps to the Fossil Shop. Turn right into Coombe Street.

Coombe Street
Coombe Street is lined with a pleasing medley of mainly 18th/19th century buildings, several of them listed, some open as galleries. Turn left at the Ship Inn to visit the Town Mill.

The Town Mill
There has been a mill on this site since at least 1340. It was severely damaged during the Civil War, but rebuilt shortly after. Commercial milling ended in 1926, but the derelict mill was eventually saved from demolition and restored to working order in 2001.

Guided tours of this fascinating watermill show how the restored Victorian milling machinery and the modern hydroelectric plant work. Each stage of the milling process is thoroughly explained and visitors can buy the flour produced. (Call 01297 444042 or visit www.townmill.org.uk to check opening times and milling days).

Other restored mill buildings nestle around the cobbled mill courtyard, housing two galleries, artisans, a café and a brewery offering craft beers. The galleries host exhibitions, primarily of local artists, both new and established and often give visitors an opportunity to meet the artists themselves. Equally, the artisans' workshops, which included a jeweller/silversmith, potters, a dressmaker and a shop specializing in seaweed designs and artworks at the time of writing, are a chance to meet, talk to and learn from craftspeople.

The Town Mill.

Caroline Smith at the Town Mill.

Dinosaurland
Return to Coombe Street and turn left for Dinosaurland and its spectacular collection of over 16,000 fossils, many collected by the owner, palaeontologist Steve Davies, and his wife Jenny. Steve describes Dinosaurland as a traditional museum, which aims "to show just how exciting and wonderful the world of fossils and dinosaurs really is."

Well-presented and labelled, the huge Fossil Collection takes up most of the ground floor of the building; the Grade 1 listed former Congregational church where Mary Anning worshipped. The collection includes a full range of local Jurassic marine fossils from the largest ichthyosaur (an extinct reptile) to ammonites, belemnites (21 varieties), fish and starfish down to the tiniest microfossil. Many specimens have extraordinary natural beauty and symmetry. Upstairs, the Time Gallery gives a vivid impression of the vastness of geological time and the Earth's history. Finally, the Natural History Room uses modern shells and skeletons to show change and continuity between the Jurassic and the present. (Dinosaurland 01297 443541 www.dinosaurland.co.uk)

Mill Green, Riverside Walk, Monmouth Street and the Church
Turn right out of Dinosaurland along Coombe Street and bear right into Mill Green. Many of the handsome 18/19th century buildings are listed and appear much as they would have done to Mary Anning and Jane Austen. Retrace your footsteps down Mill Green into Riverside Walk, which brings you back to the Mill. Turn right back into Coombe Street, then left into Monmouth Street to the parish church. Mary Anning's grave is on the left of the church path, which leads to a spectacular view east along the Jurassic Coast.

Broad Street
Retrace your steps to Bridge Street and turn right up Broad Street, which is lined with shops, including the Old Forge Fossil Shop, whilst Jurassic Gems is on the right in Drakes Way. Jane Austen is thought to have stayed at Pyne House on the left near the foot of the hill (it bears a blue plaque). Further up is the Royal Lion Hotel, parts of which are 16th century.

Charmouth Beach.

Charmouth

Charmouth Beach
Charmouth's long, family friendly beach is divided in two by the River Char, and joined with a footbridge by the car park. Both east and west beaches are pebbly at high tide, but low tide reveals more sand. Watersports, including paddleboarding, fishing, kayaking, boating and (in winter) surfing, are popular, as is collecting loose fossils. (*Hammering and digging into the cliffs are not permitted).

Charmouth Heritage Coast Centre
The centre provides information on fossils, fossil hunting and local wildlife, plus fossil collecting and rockpooling walks throughout the year. Its remarkable fossil collections showcase recent finds and the stories behind them. Outstanding is the cast of the dinosaur Scelidosaurus. At the time of writing, the ichthyosaur featured in BBC's documentary "Attenborough and the Sea Dragon" was on display too. Other fossils include splendid ammonites and a woolly mammoth tooth discovered by an eight year old boy.

There is also a film clip in which David Attenborough talks about the ichthyosaur and further films on fossils and geology and Dorset's marine life, plus an excellent collection of archive photographs. (01297 560772 https://charmouth.org, free entry).

Beneath the Heritage Centre are a café and the Charmouth Fossil Shop, with an impressive range of local and imported fossils. Of special note is the ichthyosaur skull discovered in 2000 on the beach. Next door is the Sea Lily Gallery, featuring driftwood sculptures and jewellery with a maritime flavour.

Exploring Charmouth

Charmouth's most prominent feature now, as throughout its history, is its main axis, The Street, originally part of a Roman road which connected Exeter, Dorchester and Salisbury. Recovering from devastating Viking raids, the worst but not the last of which came in 833 and 840, Charmouth grew, like Lyme, with the salt trade and fishing. In Domesday (1086) 22 households and 16 salt workers were recorded. The town was granted a market and fair in 1278 and became a borough in 1297.

Charmouth entered its golden age in 1758 with the completion of the Western Turnpike. Seven or eight coaches passed daily through The Street, where passengers changed for Lyme. Two historic buildings of note on The Street are the George, a former coaching inn and Abbot's House Restaurant opposite, where a plaque informs visitors Charles II slept there September 22-23, 1651 following his escape from defeat at the Battle of Worcester. He planned to take ship to St Malo with local shipmaster, Stephen Limbry. Hearing of this, Limbry's wife locked her husband in their bedroom and stole his clothes. Charles escaped eastwards, pursued by troops. There is also a memorial to Charles's escape later that day (23 September) in Lee Lane, Bridport. After further adventures, Charles eventually managed to escape to France from Shoreham, Sussex.

Paddleboarding, Charmouth.

Charmouth Fossil Shop.

Charmouth Beach.

Whitchurch Canonicorum

A short diversion north from the A35 leads to Whitchurch Canonicorum's impressive church. Dedicated to St Wite, it contains her shrine; an inscribed leaden casket containing the bones of a woman aged about forty. These are thought to be the only ancient relics in England apart from those of Edward the Confessor in Westminster to have survived the Reformation. The medieval church venerated St Wite as a martyr and pilgrims came to Whitchurch to seek her aid and healing, putting their diseased limbs in the openings at the base of her shrine.

Whitchurch Canonicorum Church.

St Wite's shrine.

Statue of St Wite on tower.

Chideock, Seatown and Golden Cap

Straddling the A35, Chideock's main street is lined with handsome thatched buildings in local stone. Among the best are its two inns, The Clock House and The George. From Chideock, take the narrow lane south as signed for Seatown, which has a 2km (1¼ mile) long shingle beach and a large car park. Its historic inn, The Anchor, has a superb collection of local period and recent photographs, plus fossils and items recovered from shipwrecks.

A mile long hike from Seatown leads to the summit of Golden Cap, at 191m (630ft) the highest cliff on England's south coast and a wonderful viewpoint. This was to the advantage of both "preventives" and smugglers in the 18th and early 19th centuries, when smuggling was rife on the Dorset coast.

In 1880 Rev. T Worthington, Curate of Chideock, wrote: "There used to be 30 to 40 fishermen at Seatown ostensibly employed in their lawful avocation, but really in smuggling. Not the fishermen only, but as in other seaside places half a century ago, the inhabitants in general were implicated in this contraband traffic, of which the sin in their eyes consisted only in being found out."

Knowing this, the government stationed an exciseman nearby from 1750. In this close knit community which relied heavily on the "Free Trade" excisemen were deeply resented and one was shot dead at the top of the Anchor's stairs as he eavesdropped on smugglers below. His ghost is said to haunt the inn.

Looking towards Chideock.

Looking east from Golden Cap.

Symondsbury from Colmer's Hill.

Symondsbury

Symondsbury is a large, handsome village just west of Bridport, below Colmer's Hill. The Ilchester Arms, its Grade II* listed thatched pub, has a 15th century core with 17th century and later alterations. Beyond is the Victorian school (1868) and the cruciform 14th century church of local stone with a barrel roof built by shipwrights from West Bay. Dorset's great folklorist, John Symonds Udal, a friend of Thomas Hardy, worshipped here and is buried in the churchyard.

Behind the church is Symondsbury Estate's Manor Yard. Home to a variety of interesting shops, a café/restaurant and artisan workshops, it has free parking and is a delight to explore. The contemporary gallery housed in the Grade II listed 18th century former stables features art in various media from local artists, both new and established, including ceramics, wood carvings, textiles, photography and glass. The functions venue is converted from a medieval tithe barn.

Colmer's Hill

Prominent from many angles for miles around, this near conical sandstone hill is topped by Scots pines, planted during the First World War. The modest effort of climbing to the 126m (417ft) summit is rewarded with a splendid panorama of the coast and Marshwood Vale, plus aerial views of Symondsbury and Bridport. Start from Manor Yard's car park and follow the well signed permissive path. Gentle at first, this rises steeply to the top. Follow the path down the southern slope, then left to meet the lane. Turn right to the church and left to the start.

Colmer's Hill.

Bridport from Colmer's Hill.

Bridport

Bridport began in 878AD as one of the burhs (fortified settlements) established across Wessex by King Alfred the Great in response to the ever present threat of Viking attacks. Built around the southern end of South Street, the burh was surrounded by a rampart of earth and probably surmounted with a timber palisade. It is possible a castle was built within these ramparts, either during the Saxon period or soon after the Norman Conquest, but there is no archaeological evidence to confirm this.

However, Bridport's coat of arms shows the supposed castle and what appears to be a portcullis, but is actually the spinning cogs for Bridport's mainstay, making rope. Two possible sites for the castle are in South Street. Both are occupied by late medieval houses, the Chantry (page 30) and the Castle, home of Bridport Museum (page 28).

Trade was essential to Bridport from its foundation, its name signifying "market or harbour belonging to Bredy". A mint was established there during Athelstan's reign (925-939), along with mints at Wareham, Dorchester and Shaftesbury. Dorset minted coins have been discovered in Scandinavia, giving further proof of Viking raiding and trading.

Stimulated by the demand for rope made from locally grown flax and hemp, Bridport expanded during the 13th century, a time of population growth across England. In 1213 King John ordered that there be made at Bridport "by night and day as many ropes for ships both large and small and as many cables as you can" to support his Navy. Later, Henry VIII ordered all ropes and cordage produced within five miles of Bridport must be reserved for the Navy. Sailing ships required huge quantities of rope for sails, shrouds and tackle, later for securing guns in position too. Thus Bridport's industrial prosperity was secured – with a grisly side line in supplying rope for hangmen's nooses: hence the phrase "stabbed by a Bridport dagger", a species of gallows humour said to have amused Henry VIII.

Henry III granted Bridport its first Royal Charter in 1253. Its boundaries were extended, with three wide principal streets (South, East and West Streets) meeting at a T junction as they do today. Many of the long alleyways leading off the main streets were used as ropewalks to spin rope. (The museum offers practical demonstrations of making rope, page 28).

Edward I gave Bridport the right to return two MPs and Elizabeth I granted Bridport the right to hold three annual fairs and a Saturday market. In 1593 the "market house and scole house" were built on the site of the present Georgian Town Hall.

Also crucial to Bridport's development and prosperity was its harbour. Ships were sailing up the river Brit as far as the borough by 1280 and grants were made for Bridport's harbour in 1388, 1392 and again in the 1440s. In 1670, Charles II granted powers to repair the old harbour, which was always prone to silting up. Seaborne trade was severely hampered and the problem was not truly solved until the creation of an artificial harbour at West Bay in 1740-43 (page 33), which boosted trade greatly.

The town hall.

Bridport and Lyme were much involved in emigration to North America, especially Newfoundland. Many local people sailed to New England between 1620 and 1650, evidenced in place names, including Bridport, Vermont; Bridport Inlet (North West Territories, Canada); and the towns of Lyme in Connecticut, New York and New Hampshire.

Bridport and the Monmouth Rebellion, 1685
Although Bridport did not suffer as many casualties or as much damage as Lyme during the Civil War, it was the scene of conflict in 1685. On 13th June, only two days after landing at Lyme (page 7), Monmouth sent 300 men to Bridport under Lord Grey and Lt. Colonel Venner to confront a group of militia who were camped just east of the town to intercept his communications. Grey and Venner met little resistance until they reached the Bull Inn, East Street, where Militia Deputy Lieutenants Edward Coker and Wadham Strangways were billeted. When Coker shot Venner "in the belly" from his bedroom window, the rebels stormed the Bull and Venner killed Coker, whose memorial may be seen in St Mary's Church, South Street (page 29). Strangways also died in the fight. Monmouth's men attacked a militia barrier at the end of East Street. Two men were killed, others taken prisoner and Lord Grey's horse was shot. The wounded Venner ordered a retreat.

The Bull Hotel.

Rope and Bridport's Prosperity
After the religiously fuelled turmoil of the 17th century, Bridport entered a long period of growth thanks largely to the expanding demand from naval and merchant ships for rope. Bridport's many fine Georgian and Victorian buildings testify to its prosperity, as does the handsome Town Hall of 1786, the factories and many humbler workers' houses.

In the late 18th century, 1,800 of Bridport's 3,100 inhabitants are said to have worked in the rope and related net industries, with a further 7,000 employed in the surrounding towns and villages. Sailcloth was a related industry. It was woven in and around Bridport, first as a home based industry and then in factories with machinery from the mid-19th century. Similarly, net making machinery was introduced in Victoria's reign, though some nets were still made by hand into the 20th century. Court Mills off West Street, Bridport's earliest factory site, is the largest textile mill complex in Dorset. Further industrial areas of Bridport include North Mills, Priory Mills and Pymore Mills.

Bridport's Industrial Heritage

That so much of Bridport's solid industrial architecture survives is unusual in Britain and something well worth preserving. This survival is partly due to many former warehouses and mills being among the 514 listed buildings in the town. Some former warehouses and mills have been repurposed as apartments as at West Mill, West Street or as new businesses such as St Michael's Centre, St Michael's Lane, but have retained their essential industrial character. Some others (including part of Court Mills) are still used in the rope and net making industries. Although nylon has replaced hemp as the raw material, Bridport retains an important industrial position, especially in the production of military netting and netting for tennis and football.

Bridport today
Bridport is a lively town with street markets on Saturday and Wednesday and a monthly farmers' market, plus monthly markets for antiques and books, arts and crafts, vinyl records, artisanal products and a summer market in West Bay. There is a wide range of shops to browse and if you're looking for something unusual, Bridport is a likely place to find it. Many are independent businesses, including shops for antiques, clothes, music, plus several art galleries and bookshops. Some are new, others long established: RJ Balson and Sons at West Allington (just beyond West Street), England's oldest family butchers, has been trading since 1515.

Bridport also has a vibrant arts scene, with its own arts centre, two theatres, a cinema and museum, plus an annual Literary Festival with a highly regarded prize. As well as its several advantages, many incomers are attracted by the town's cultural ambience, boosted by a number of artists and writers who have made Bridport their home

Four scenes from Bridport's market.

East Street, Bridport.

Bridport Town Hall
Centrally placed where South, East and West Streets meet, Bridport's handsome Georgian Town Hall is also the Tourist Information Centre and the best place to start exploring the town. A Grade 1 listed building, it was constructed of local red brick and Portland stone in 1786 for £2,000 on the site of St Andrew's Chapel after fire had destroyed the original market house. The distinctive clock and cupola were added twenty years later. Entry is free. Paintings by Fra Newberry (1855-1946) depicting Bridport rope and net making are on permanent display along with memorabilia from the two ships called HMS Bridport.

South Street
Facing the Town Hall is the mysteriously named Bucky Doo Square, where visitors enjoy live music most Saturdays – the chief market day when Bridport's main streets are lined with stalls. On the left is the Arts Centre, housed in the handsome former Methodist chapel of 1838. Its theatre is a fine venue for plays, film, dance, comedy and music. Upstairs, the Allsop Gallery, a large, airy, well-lit space, hosts regular exhibitions, particularly by local artists. Bridport Museum occupies the Castle, a Grade II* listed early 16th century building of hammer dressed stone with ashlar dressings and mullioned windows. It gives a comprehensive introduction to Bridport and its history with a very wide range of exhibits. Archive photographs vividly tell the story of rope and net making, alongside many plaques to explain the various processes involved. Practical demonstrations are given on a 150 year old hand driven rope jack and there is also a Bridport built jumper loom on display.

Local life in and around Bridport, including seaside holidays at West Bay, is also told through archive photographs, with spoken testimony at the oral history booth. Other collections include fossils and geology and archaeology, with finds from several periods, notably prehistoric and Roman. Historic maps show how Bridport has grown, but also how constant its street pattern has been. There are good sections on art, trade, railways and shipping too. Dr Roberts' medical collection includes some remarkable treatments based on locally sourced ingredients such as spiders and excrement of dog.

Walk down South Street to the Electric Palace, a venue for cinema and a variety of live entertainment. Dating from 1926, it has been well restored with an elegant Art Deco interior and particularly fine murals. St Mary's, Bridport's parish church, dates largely from rebuilding in 1397, but much of the north and south transepts are from its Norman predecessor. Across the street is the Quaker Meeting House, at least late 17th century in origin, though much altered in the 18th century. Beyond is a fine collection of 18th/early 19th century buildings, all different, but making a harmonious whole.

Back on the west side of the street is the far older Chantry. Bridport's oldest domestic building, it is easily overlooked because of its modern tiles and Victorian windows. Probably dating from the 14th or 15th century, it was once known as the "Prior's House", but more likely belonged to a chantry priest.

Palmer's, the only thatched brewery in England, is half a mile from the Chantry, just beyond the roundabout in West Bay Road. Founded in

Palmer's Brewery.

The Chapel in the Garden.

The Chantry.

1794 by the local Gundry family, who first made their money in rope and net, the brewery is best viewed by turning into Skilling Hill Road, crossing the handsome iron bridge (don't miss the Stalking Dog sculpture opposite) and heading down the riverbank path. Originally, the brewery was water powered and its waterwheel was forged in Bridport in 1879. Brewing continues on traditional lines, using top fermenting yeast, a mash tun and open top copper. All this and much more about the brewing process is revealed on the brewery tour (book in advance 01308 422396 www.palmersbrewery.com).

East Street
Next to the Town Hall is the Greyhound Hotel, built in the 18th century, but altered in the 19th. Continue to the Bull Hotel, scene of bloodshed in 1685 (page 25). Although it dates from the 17th century, its street front, like that of the Greyhound, is typical of the 19th century. Beyond on the north side at number 49 is the attractive Chapel in the Garden, which traces its Independent congregation back to 1672. The handsome Literary and Scientific Institute, number 51, was built in Portland Stone in 1855.

Divert left up Barack Street to visit the Lyric Theatre. First built as a chapel in 1742, it was later Bridport's first cinema, then a theatre. Venue for artists and the Puppet Club, it is one of many places in Bridport to host exhibitions during Dorset Arts Week, one of the largest open studios events in the country. Its strikingly decorated doors were painted by young local artists Imi Neylan and Marina Renee-Cemmick. Further up Barrack Street is the sober stone built Port Bredy Hospital, a former workhouse of 1836, converted to housing in 1999.

Its name refers to Thomas Hardy, who called Bridport "Port Bredy" in his story "Fellow Townsmen" from "Wessex Tales", which is clearly set in Bridport. The main character, Barnet, is the son of a wealthy rope merchant and many local places are easily recognizable, including West Bay, the harbour, beaches and cliffs; the Bull Hotel and the Town Hall.

Hardy describes the closeness of the countryside and rural life to Bridport in the story: "The shepherd on the east hill could shout out lambing intelligence to the shepherd on the west hill, over the intervening town chimneys without great inconvenience to his voice, so nearly did the steep pastures encroach upon the burghers' backyards. And at night it was possible to stand in the very midst of the town and hear from their native paddocks on the lower levels of the greensward the mild lowing of the farmer's heifers…."

West Street

Bridport and traffic noise have grown considerably since Hardy wrote Fellow Townsmen in 1880, but the countryside is still close and there is a fine view of Colmer's Hill as you look down West Street from the Town Hall. Look back as you head down West Street for a different angle on the Town Hall.

On the left is The Ropemakers, with a good sign depicting Bridport's chief industry. The inn was built in the late 18th century by the Gundry family and originally called The Sun. Across the road on Victoria Grove corner is a solid three storey stone building. Built in 1844 as a warehouse, it is part of Gundry's Court Mills, which has produced cordage and netting since 1665. Further down West Street is West Mill, a late 19th century red brick building with Portland stone dressings and a projecting sack hoist on the top floor.

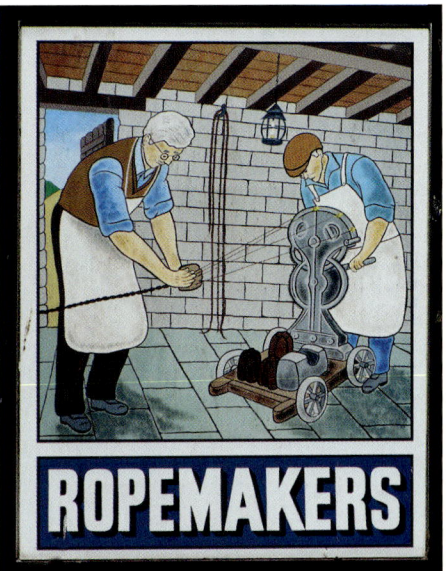

Cross the bridge. Just beyond The White Lion, formerly called The Tanners after Bridport's tannery, is RJ Balson and Son, England's oldest family butchers. Turn right into North Allington and cross St Swithun's Road to visit St Swithun's 1827 neo-Grecian style church. Retrace your steps up West Street past West Mill. Turn right by the Cornish Pasty Shop into unsigned St Michael's Lane to visit St Michael's Centre, a delightful place to browse for arts, crafts and curios.

Among items on sale are a huge range of textiles, plus books, paintings, ceramics, toys, clothes and cards.

Cross into Ropewalks car park. On the left the long, narrow rope walks, originally burgage plots for the houses on West Street, are easy to discern. One leads back to The Ropemakers. Turn right at the end of the car park (still Ropewalks) past Stephen Whetman's huge warehouse to Gundry Lane. Turn left past the Local History Centre and Whetman's coach house to visit Borough Gardens. Turn left up Gundry Lane and left again up South Street to the Town Hall.

Live music at Bridport market.

The Lyric Theatre.

Bridport Arts Centre.

West Bay (Bridport's harbour)

Always prone to silting up, the River Brit was far from ideal for shipping and over the centuries there were several attempts to build a harbour at what is now West Bay. The need for a harbour at the river's mouth was not really solved until 1740, when two piers were built and the River Brit was diverted to run between them. A sluice gate was erected at the mouth of the river to control the flow of water into the harbour so that the tide would scour it of sand and silt. Trade improved dramatically, and harbour dues rose correspondingly from £18 in 1743 when the harbour re-opened to £800 in 1773. Between 1807 and 1818 the original wooden piers were almost completely rebuilt and extended. In 1823 a new Act of Parliament was obtained to completely rebuild the harbour to accommodate growing trade. A new basin was dug and lined with stone; the piers were rebuilt, first in wood, then, in 1866, in stone and a new road was engineered from the harbour to Bridport. The number of ships doubled in three years and in 1832 Bridport became a bond port with its own customs house.

Shipbuilding also prospered at Bridport, with 13 acres of shipyards employing up to 300 people. Between 1769 and 1879, these yards built 353 vessels, including 18 ships for the Navy during the Napoleonic Wars. Cutters, brigantines, barques, brigs, clippers, frigates, ketches, luggers, schooners and smacks were some of the vessels built at West Bay. The largest was the clipper *Speedy*, completed in 1853. At 1002 tons she was slightly larger than

View west from East Cliff.

West Bay harbour showing Pier Terrace.

the famous *Cutty Sark*, 963 tons. However, iron ships were replacing wooden ones and the last ship built at Bridport Harbour was in 1879.

Bridport harbour's commercial heyday was short lived. The railway reached Bridport in 1857, with an extension to the harbour in 1884, diverting much freight to rail. Bridport further lost trade as cargo ships grew bigger and needed larger port facilities and deeper water. In 1881 Bridport lost its bond port status.

In 1884 the Great Western Railway named the harbour "West Bay" to attract tourists, emphasizing its changed status and purpose as a seaside holiday destination. That year, West Bay's most notable building, Pier Terrace, was built in the Arts and Crafts style by Edward Schroeder Prior.

As at Lyme, genteel visitors had been visiting Bridport and West Bay in modest numbers since the late 18th century. According to the 1792 summer edition of St James' Chronicle: "Bridport is a clean, well-built small town…All the conveniences and comforts, indeed the luxuries of life, are obtainable here…there is excellent bathing…."

The railway brought cheap mass transport to West Bay as it did later at Lyme (page 9), popularizing the resort in an era when increasing numbers of working people could afford a holiday by the sea. Although the station closed to passengers in 1930 and to freight in 1962, the rise of the motor car ensured West Bay's prosperity.

West Bay's beaches

West Bay's two beaches are separated by the harbour. Both are popular with families and there is plenty to do from swimming (please beware of strong currents and a steep shelf), to beach fishing, paddleboarding, kayaking and boating.

East Beach is backed by beautiful golden sandstone cliffs. Lifeguarded in the summer season, it has coarse sand and small pebbles. It also has ample space. At low tide, it is continuous with Hive and Cogden beaches (page 38), which may be accessed by road or by the Coastpath. The views, including the aerial view of West Bay from East Cliff, are superb but the walk to Hive Beach is a hearty 2¾ miles (4.3km) and the climb up East Cliff is steep.

West Beach is slightly further from West Bay's many facilities than East Beach. A long beach with pebbles and some sand at low tide, it is continuous with the beach at Eype Mouth when the tide is out.

Gig racing at West Bay.

East Cliff, West Bay.

Eype Mouth

The long pebble beach at Eype Mouth is also accessible from West Bay by the Coastpath, a fairly demanding 1¼ mile (2.1km) walk with a long ascent and descent. To drive there, use the narrow lane signed from the A35 through the attractive village of Lower Eype (which has a pub and a hotel) and use the beach car park. Access to the beach itself is short and easy, though stepped. The views are wonderful and the beach refreshingly simple and uncommercialized.

Exploring West Bay's Harbour

Start from the long stay car park in West Bay Road, where the former railway station is a restaurant, the Station Kitchen, with a converted railway carriage and a short section of track. Opposite is Slader's Yard, a private art gallery exhibiting and selling contemporary British art, including handmade furniture and designer craft.

Head down West Bay Road towards the harbour. Across the car park is West Bay Discovery Centre. A small, family friendly museum with interactive displays aimed at children, it is housed in the Grade II listed former Methodist chapel. The Discovery Centre's artefacts and archive photographs provide a good insight into West Bay's history from its shipbuilding heyday to its reinvention as a Victorian resort and recent fame as the location for the television drama, Broadchurch. Talks, guided walks and events are also offered by the centre (01308 427288).

West Bay harbour.

Opposite is the Bridport Arms Hotel, two thatched blocks from the 17th and 18th centuries linked by a modern hotel. Inside is a remarkable collection of local period photographs. Those of sailing boats in West Bay are especially interesting, as are the portraits of sailors and fishermen.

East Beach is behind the hotel. For a good view of the golden sandstone cliffs, follow the quay by Pier Terrace past the lobster pots and fishing nets to the end. Take a stroll around West Bay's harbour, which is at its best at high tide on a summer's evening, when the pleasing medley of fishing boats and leisure craft is highlighted by the mellow sun and colours reflect richly in the water. There's a wide range of refreshments: pubs, cafés (some specializing in seafood); ice cream and fish and chips.

The harbour is of considerable historic interest and a listed building in its own right. It consists of two parallel moles of huge ashlar blocks, partly revetted with iron and supported with concrete. Other sections of the harbour walls have huge timber piles, some with iron driving rings round the top, instead of the iron revetments. This is heaven for those who love the water. Paddleboards, canoes and boats can be hired. There are opportunities to go on river and coastal trips, water skiing, wakeboarding, wreck and mackerel fishing.

Cross the weir where sluice gates control the flow of water to the harbour. Across the road is a large stone shed with black doors. This is the Old Salt House, where salt was stored for the local and Newfoundland fishing

West Bay harbour.

trades. From Tudor times, Dorset was deeply involved in fishing cod on the teeming Newfoundland Banks and many Newfoundlanders can trace their ancestry to Dorset.

Continue around the harbour. Opposite is Pier Terrace (1884). At the end of the pier is another connection with Canada. A plaque recalls the Yukon Exercises, rehearsals by mainly Canadian troops for the ill-fated Dieppe Raid of 1942, which were conducted on this section of the Dorset coast because of its striking similarity to the beaches and harbour across the Channel at Dieppe.

Hive Beach.

Burton Bradstock
Burton Bradstock is an exceptionally attractive village three miles east of Bridport on the B3157. It has two good pubs, The Anchor and The Three Horseshoes, and a medieval church. The village's stone built houses, many of them thatched, are prettily arranged around a network of lanes, all a delight to explore on foot.

Hive and Cogden Beaches
The turning for Hive Beach and the National Trust car park is just beyond Burton Bradstock. A long stretch of steeply shelving shingle, Hive Beach is continuous with neighbouring Cogden Beach. Beach fishing is popular, as is fossil hunting, boating, kayaking and sailboarding. Please heed posted warnings of the strong tides and undertow if swimming or going out on the water. The beach has a large café, toilets and a Coastwatch station.

Burton Bradstock.

Calendar of Main Events in Lyme and Bridport

This is only a selection from the many events held in Lyme and Bridport. Contact Tourist Information at Bridport Town Hall 01308 424901 or at Church Street, Lyme Regis 01297 442138 for up to date information, dates and times. Also recommended are the monthly farmers' markets in Lyme and Bridport and Saturday and Wednesday street markets in Bridport.

May: Lyme Festival of Jazz, Blues and Soul; Lyme May Fete; Lyme Fossil Festival
June: Bridport Food Festival
July: Bridport Charter Fair; Jurassic Fields Music Festival; Lyme Summer Show; Lyme Regis Lifeboat Week
August: Bridport Open Studios; Bridport Folk Festival; Melplash Agriculture Show; Lyme Regis Beer Festival; Lyme Folk Weekend; Lyme Carnival and Regatta
September: Bridport Hat Festival
November: Bridport Literary Festival

Useful websites include:
lovelymeregis.co.uk, whatsoninlyme.co.uk, lymeregis.org
bridportandwestbay.co.uk, westbay.co.uk and bridportnews.co.uk.

Two interesting walks

The following pages detail two walks in the area covered by this guide; one is an exploration of Lyme and the surrounding region, the other takes in some of the glorious scenery of the coast.

A walk around Lyme Regis

Distance: 8km/5miles, Time: 2½ hours, Map: OS Explorer 116.

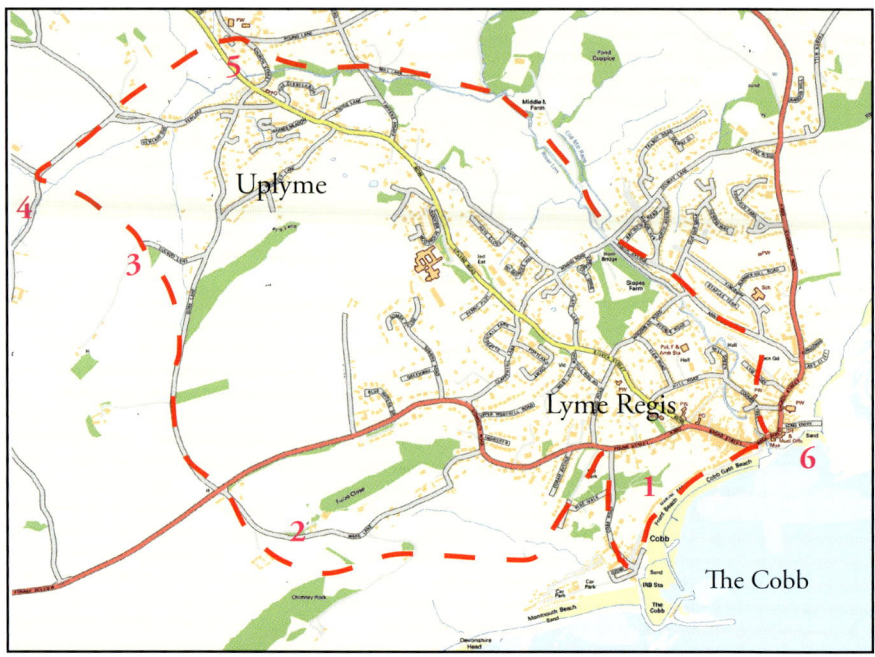

Information
Start: Holmbush car park, Lyme Regis DT7 3HX, SY337920.
Terrain: Footpaths, quiet lanes and back streets. Two short, steep ascents, one steep descent. **Stiles:** 8.
Refreshments: Pub in Uplyme; wide choice of pubs, cafés and restaurants in Lyme Regis.
Public toilets: At start and in Lyme.

Packed with interest and variety, this circuit of Lyme Regis includes superb views of Dorset's Jurassic Coast and a visit to the Undercliffs, part of the area's remarkable geology that made it Britain's first natural World Heritage Site. Lyme Regis has a particularly rich fossil heritage, which can be explored in its excellent museums. Also en route is Lyme Fossil Shop; the Cobb - Lyme's medieval breakwater – and a restored watermill. Take time to enjoy these, the resort's timeless air and its many extant Georgian buildings, which would be instantly recognizable to the characters of Jane Austen's *Persuasion* and John Fowles' *The French Lieutenant's Woman*.

1. Walk to the lower end of Holmbush car park and join the signed Coast Path. Continue ahead signed "Ware ½" when you reach a path junction. Only 100m ahead, bear left "To Coast Path". Keep ahead "Coast Path Seaton" at the next signpost. Good views onto the Jurassic Coast and the Cobb open out. Spring flowers, including ragged robin, bluebells, bird's foot trefoil and orchids thrive here. Continue on the Coast Path into the Axmouth-Lyme Regis Undercliffs. Turn right "Permissive Path to Chimney Rock". The path winds gently through trees, then climbs steeply up steps to Chimney Rock, a remnant stack of Chert Beds rock. Continue up more steps. Follow the field path ahead to a stile. Continue to a lane and bear left.

2. Follow the lane to the main road. Cross with care into Gore Lane. After 400m, bear left onto a signed "Public Footpath". Follow the path to a stile. Turn right along the edge of the field. Follow the path steeply downhill to a lane by a house.

3. Turn left. Only 50m ahead, turn right at a junction of paths to cross a stile. Take the signed public footpath almost immediately left. This heads north-west, leading over another stile and the bed of a dismantled railway. Continue downhill to meet a lane at a metal five barred gate. On your left, at a distance of some 500m, are the tall arches of the dismantled railway, the 1903 Axminster to Lyme Regis branch line.

4. Turn right and follow the lane ahead for 450m ignoring side turnings. Fork left. Cross a lane into a drive. Turn right 30m ahead into a public footpath. Continue with the hedge on your left. Follow the edge of the cricket field to the main road. Cross carefully and climb the steps ahead to the church, where the ancient churchyard yew is said to be 1,000 years old.

5. Turn right and downhill opposite the church. Only 100m ahead, turn left into a signed public footpath beside the River Lim. Cross the lane ahead and continue into Mill Lane. Continue ahead at the next path junction. The path follows the Lim past a cottage with a waterwheel and crosses a footbridge. Again continue ahead, now with the river on your right. Follow the signs into Lyme Regis. Turn left as signed for Dinosaurland Fossil Museum and Lyme Regis Museum. Some 50m beyond Dinosaurland in Coombe Street is the Town Mill. Continue down Coombe Street to visit Lyme Fossil Shop and Lyme Regis Museum.

6. Turn right and follow the Coastpath into Marine Parade to the Cobb. Take time to explore the Cobb, with its RNLI station and aquarium. Follow the lane uphill from the Cobb to the car park.

Seatown and Golden Cap - *Distance: 3½ miles/5.5km, Time: 2 hours, Maps: OS Explorer 116, Landranger 193.*

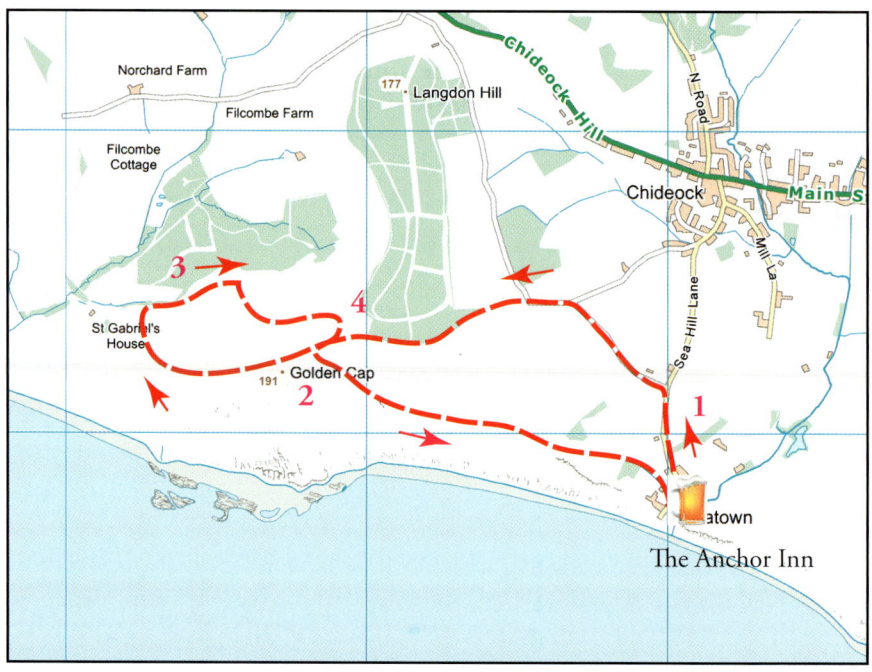

Start/parking: Seatown, SY420917, DT6 6JU.
Terrain: Footpaths, tracks and short section of lane. Attention needed to directions. Two steep ascents and descents.
Stiles: 1. **Public Toilets:** At start.

Golden Cap, the highlight of this demanding but very rewarding walk, is a massive cliff of Jurassic strata. At 630ft (191m), it is the highest cliff on England's south coast. The views are magnificent: east along Chesil Bank to Portland Bill and westwards across Lyme Bay. Seatown's Anchor Inn has a huge collection of local photographs, plus fossils and items recovered from shipwrecks. En route is the ruined church of Stanton St Gabriel, reputedly used to stash contraband brandy after its closure in 1800.

1. Start: Head up the lane from the Anchor Inn for 450m. Turn left, signed "Langdon Woods". Climb steadily. When the path divides, continue ahead, signed "Coast Path Golden Cap".
2. 1 mile/1.9km Follow the Coast Path along the summit of Golden Cap and then steeply downhill via steps to a gate. Turn diagonally right, signed "St

Gabriel's". At the path junction below, bear left at a signpost "St Gabriel's". The ruined church is 50m ahead. Retrace your steps to the signpost.

3. 1¾ miles/2.8km Continue ahead, signed "Langdon Wood Seatown". Head steeply up the slope, aiming for a small gate and a fingerpost with three arms. Care is needed at this point because the arms are poorly aligned. Continue in the same direction over the shoulder of the rise ahead, ie east-south-east - a more easterly course than indicated by the "Langdon Wood" sign.

4. 2¼ miles/3.7km At the next fingerpost, turn sharp right, signed "Golden Cap". Retrace the first part of the route, but only for 200m to the next stile and gate. Turn left and left again to join the Coast Path. Follow it downhill to Seatown. Turn right to the start.

Select Bibliography
Fowles, John: *A Short History of Lyme Regis*, Dovecote Press, Wimborne, 1991.
Gosling, Gerald: *Bridport Past*, Phillimore, Chichester, 1999.
Hesketh, Robert: *A Guide to the Beaches and Coves of Dorset*, Inspiring Places Publishing, Alderholt, 2012.
Hesketh, Robert: *Tales of the Dorset Coast*, Inspiring Places Publishing, Alderholt, 2015.
Lane, Maggie, *Jane Austen and Lyme Regis*, Jane Austen Society, Chawton, 2003.
Le Pard, Gordon: *Dorset and the Sea*, Dorset Books, Wellington, 2010.

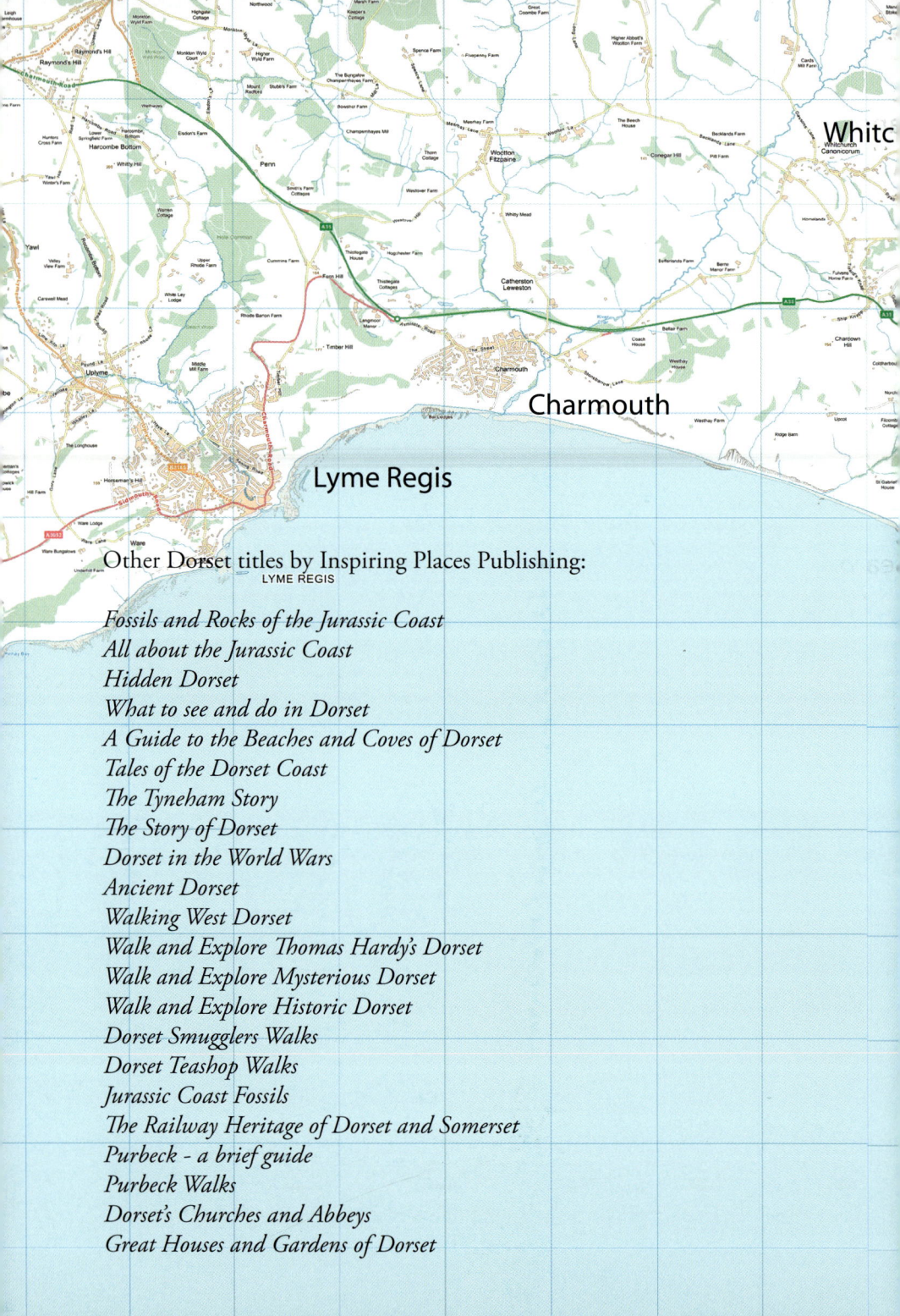

Other Dorset titles by Inspiring Places Publishing:

Fossils and Rocks of the Jurassic Coast
All about the Jurassic Coast
Hidden Dorset
What to see and do in Dorset
A Guide to the Beaches and Coves of Dorset
Tales of the Dorset Coast
The Tyneham Story
The Story of Dorset
Dorset in the World Wars
Ancient Dorset
Walking West Dorset
Walk and Explore Thomas Hardy's Dorset
Walk and Explore Mysterious Dorset
Walk and Explore Historic Dorset
Dorset Smugglers Walks
Dorset Teashop Walks
Jurassic Coast Fossils
The Railway Heritage of Dorset and Somerset
Purbeck - a brief guide
Purbeck Walks
Dorset's Churches and Abbeys
Great Houses and Gardens of Dorset